BESTIE,

I can't imagine what I would ever do without you!
You mean so much to me that I had to write a book about it.
Here are 50 reasons why you mean so much to me.

LOVE YA BUNCHES,

____

1

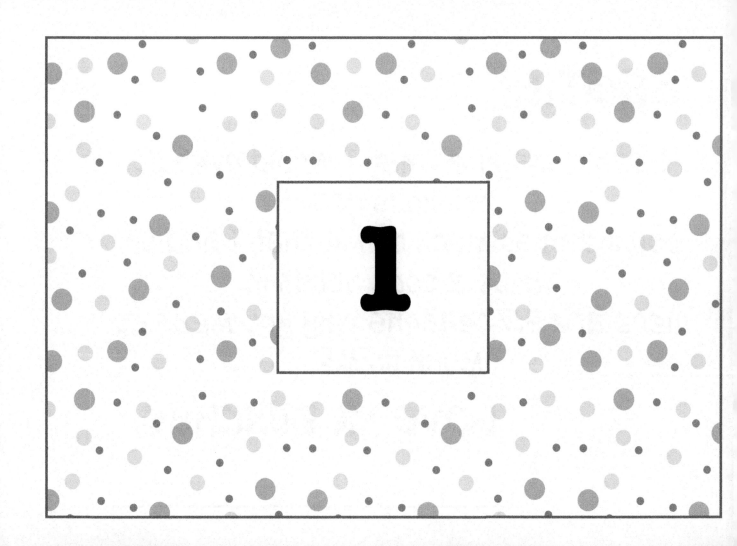

YOU ARE MY

FAVORITE

IN THE WORLD. 

2

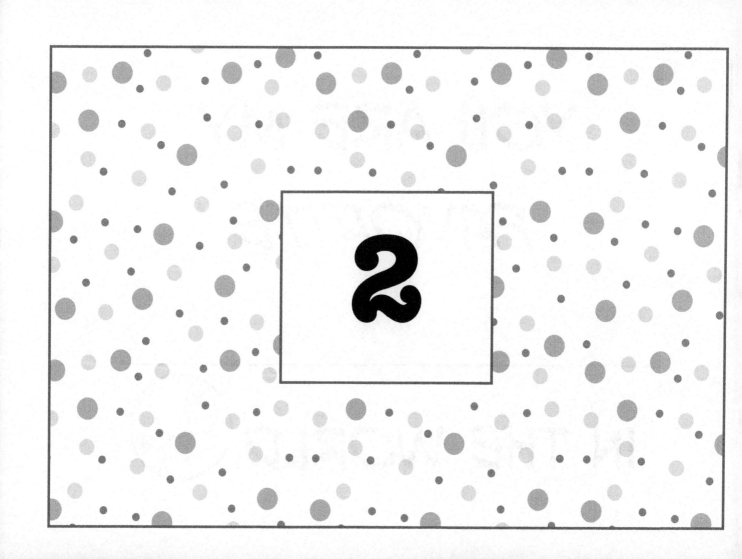

WE MAKE A GREAT TEAM JUST LIKE

____________________ &

____________________.

3

THANK YOU FOR

ALWAYS

________________________.

4

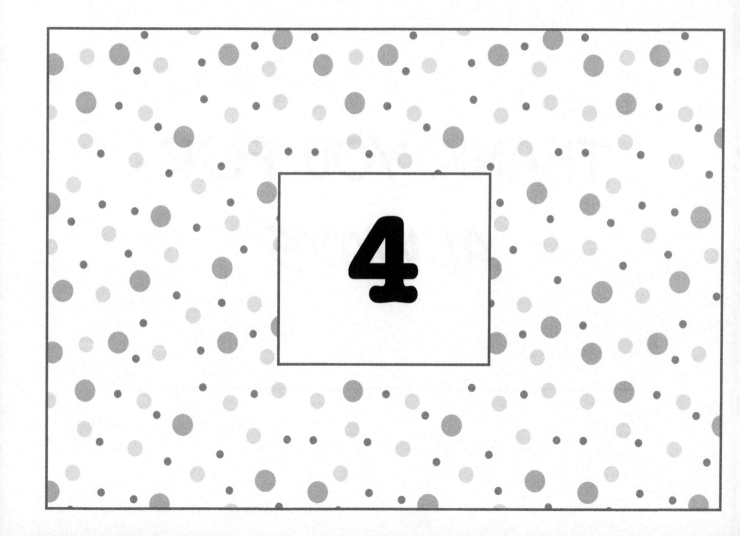

THE BEST ADVICE
YOU EVER
GAVE ME WAS

______________________.

5

MY FAVORITE
THING TO DO
WITH YOU IS

______________________________.

6

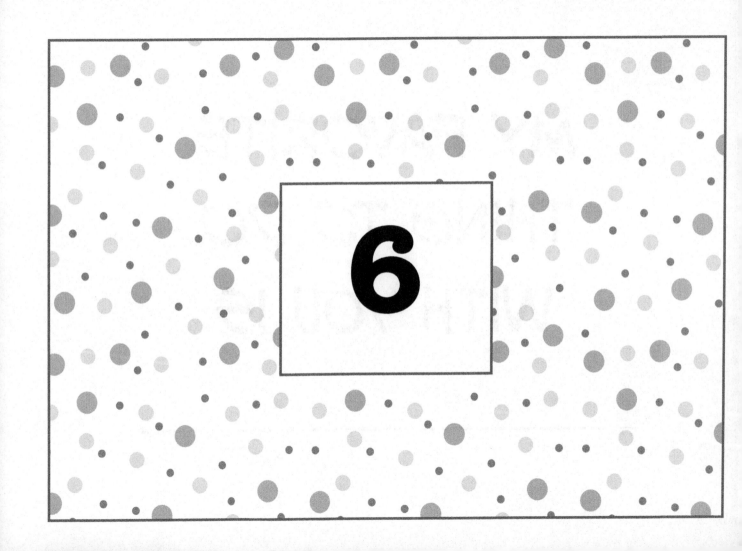

I COULD TALK
TO YOU FOR
HOURS ABOUT

______________________________.

7

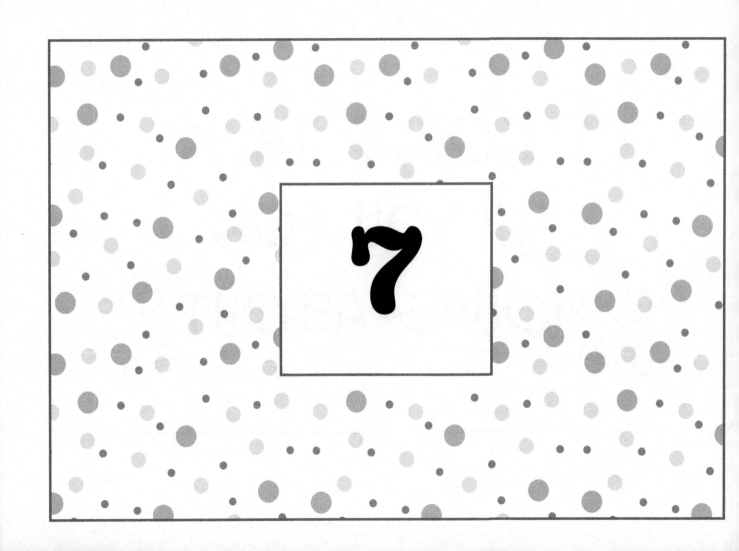

I LOVE IT WHEN YOU CALL ME

______________________.

8

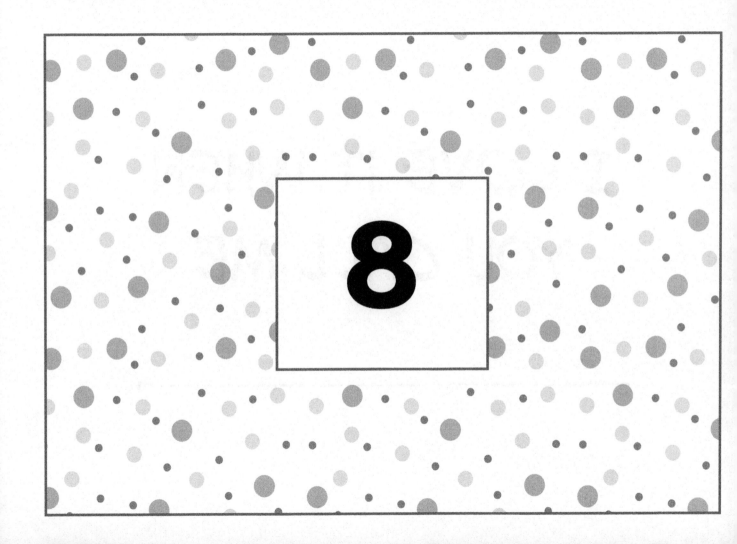

THANK YOU FOR ALWAYS TAKING MY SIDE ABOUT

______________________.

9

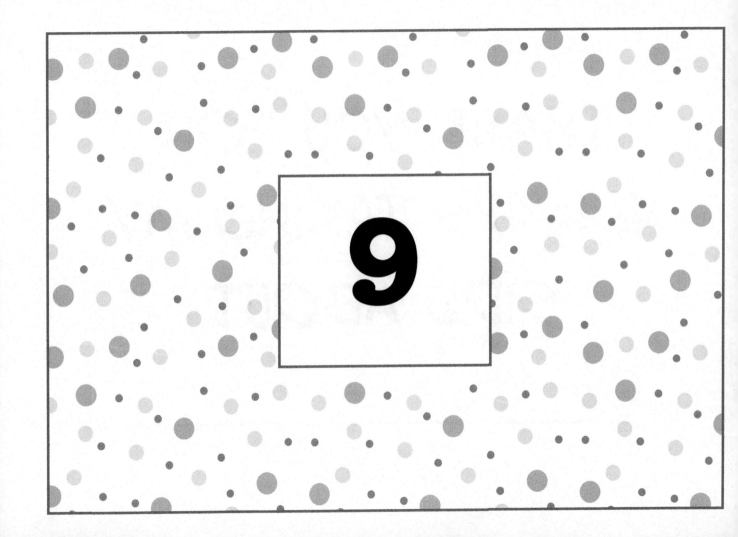

THE BEST THING ABOUT OUR FRIENDSHIP IS

________________________.

10

IF YOU WERE
A SONG IT
WOULD BE

________________________________.

11

THANK YOU
FOR NEVER
FORGETTING

______________________________.

12

THANK YOU
FOR FORGIVING
ME FOR

______________________________.

13

YOU ALWAYS MAKE EVERYONE FEEL

______________________.

14

IF YOU WERE AN ANIMAL YOU WOULD BE

________________________________.

15

THE DAY WE MET
I THOUGHT

______________________.

16

I CAN'T WAIT TO

____

WITH YOU.

17

IF YOU WERE
A COLOR IT
WOULD BE

________________________________.

18

YOU ARE THE ONLY ONE THAT CAN

______________________________.

19

EVERYONE

SHOULD BE AS

____

AS YOU.

20

YOU ARE SO
TALENTED AT

______________________________.

21

IF YOU WERE
EVER IN TROUBLE
I WOULD

______________________________.

22

MY FAVORITE MEMORY WITH YOU IS

__________________________________.

23

WHEN I'M STRESSED OUT YOU

____________________.

24

MY FAVORITE NICKNAME FOR YOU IS

______________________________.

25

I CAN'T EVEN BE **MAD** AT YOU WHEN

______________________________.

26

I LOVE
HEARING YOUR
STORIES ABOUT

______________________.

27

I WISH I
HAD KNOWN
YOU WHEN

______________________________.

28

I LOVE YOU AS MUCH AS I HATE

________________________________.

29

WHEN WE
GET OLD
I HOPE WE

________________________________.

30

I WISH YOU HAD BEEN WITH ME WHEN

______________________________.

31

YOU INSPIRE
ME TO

______________________________.

32

IF WE EVER LOST TOUCH I WOULD

________________________.

33

YOU ARE THE
FIRST ONE

I CALL WHEN

________________________________.

34

I HOPE YOU
ALWAYS REMEMBER

______________________________.

35

I LOVE THAT YOU ARE MY BEST FRIEND BECAUSE

________________________________.

36

YOU ARE SO
SMART ABOUT

______________________.

37

I WOULD LOVE TO GO ON VACATION WITH YOU TO

______________________.

38

YOU MAKE ME
A BETTER
PERSON BY

______________________.

39

YOU HAVE
THE BEST

____

EVER.

40

YOU ARE THE MOST **FUN** WHEN

______________________________.

41

I KNOW I CAN ALWAYS COUNT ON YOU TO

______________________________.

42

YOU ALWAYS MAKE ME *laugh* WHEN

______________________________.

43

IF I EVER WON THE ***LOTTERY*** I WOULD BUY YOU

______________________________.

44

THE 3 WORDS I'D
USE TO DESCRIBE
YOU ARE

____________, ____________,

& ____________.

45

YOU LOVE

____

SO MUCH IT
MAKES ME LAUGH.

46

THANK YOU FOR
NEVER TELLING
ANYONE

______________________________.

47

WHEN YOU ARE **MAD** AT ME I

______________________________.

48

THE FICTIONAL CHARACTER YOU REMIND ME OF IS

______________________.

49

WHEN I'M **SAD**
YOU CHEER ME
UP BY

______________________________.

50

I ***ALWAYS*** AGREE WITH YOU WHEN IT COMES TO

____________________________.

Made in the USA
Coppell, TX
30 October 2021

64921187R00057